STORY HYPOTHESIS

THE MISSING PIECE OF YOUR FICTION PUZZLE

JP RINDFLEISCH IX

9th Publishing
& Associates

CONTENTS

THE STORY HYPOTHESIS FORMULA

There is a rhythmic pulse to every compelling story, a heartbeat that fuels its emotional resonance and thematic depth. But often, writers can lose sight of this core. This book aims to be your compass to finding and harnessing that heartbeat, the tool that can turn a simple tale into an unforgettable journey.

The Story Hypothesis Defined

A formula for a theme using needs to define a character's overall trajectory and enhance narrative resonance.

> *[Character's] need for [Initial Want] leads them to fulfill [True Need] by developing [Developing Need].*

The needs referred to here are Manfred Max-Neef's 9 Fundamental Human Needs.

A Quick Word for the Budget-Conscious Reader

If budgetary constraints have you wondering the worth of this purchase, allow me this suggestion: take a screenshot of this introduction, especially the formula, if you're using the "look inside" feature online. Print it out and place it in your workspace.

Who is This Book For?

Writers Seeking Resonance: If you've ever dreamt of crafting stories that linger in the hearts and minds of your readers, stories that echo long after the last word is read, this book is your guide.

Writers Facing Obstacles: If your scenes feel off, or if you find yourself entangled in the maze of your story's larger purpose, this method offers the clarity to pave a way forward.

The Journey of the Story Hypothesis Formula

I've been privileged to introduce Story Hypothesis to numerous clients throughout my career. The result? That exhilarating moment when the metaphorical lightbulb illuminates, and the narrative path becomes clear. I've witnessed the transformation—from stories that meander without purpose to tales that captivate.

I hadn't originally planned on writing this, but after my ramblings on theme became clearer, and others started asking for some kind of resource, this book was born.

The Value of the Complete Journey

While this introduction gives you the essence of the formula, the chapters that follow delve deep, offering insights, techniques, and case studies that demystify Story Hypothesis.

THEME: THE THING WE WRITER'S SWEEP UNDER THE RUG

Raise your hand if you've ever thought, "Themes are pointless. There is no way they help with my writing process."

Wait, is my hand up? Whoops.

I still think that's true, to an extent. But don't ghost me just yet!

For a long time, I struggled with the concept of theme. I knew it was supposed to be important, but I just couldn't seem to make it work for me. I'm sure many of you can relate. Maybe you've tried to incorporate a theme into your writing, only to end up feeling like it's a forced and unnatural addition. Or maybe you've just avoided themes altogether, thinking they're something only English teachers and literary snobs care about.

But here's the thing: as readers, we know themes are a fundamental part of storytelling. It's more than just something to pontificate about inside a classroom and get an A over. Theme gives us the feels, it is the final tolling bell of a story that can stick with a reader for decades. So if that's true, why can't we figure out how to make it work for us as writers?

That's what I wanted to find out.

In school, they taught me that theme was the main idea or message in a story. Back then, it was easy to identify: *Romeo and Juliet* was about love. *To Kill a Mockingbird* was about friendship. But let's be real, that definition of theme is nonsense for both writers and readers. I mean, imagine recommending *The Fault in Our Stars* to someone looking for a theme on love. Unless you enjoy crushing souls (no judgment), they probably won't come to you for book recommendations again.

So, that definition sucks, but I'm not giving up. Let's see what the Oxford Dictionary has to say.

According to the good ol' Oxford, a theme is defined as "a subject of discussion or conversation; a topic."

Okay, that's something.

Instead of some airy concept, we now know that themes are a conversation and discussion between the reader and the author. They're grounded in some kind of back and forth between what the writer writes and the reader's interpretation.

With this new definition, then books like *1984* become more than the idea of totalitarianism, and more like the discussion of what governmental overreach looks like, so we critically think about what our government does. *The Lord of the Rings* becomes more than good vs. evil, and more akin to how even the smallest of people can make a difference.

That suggests to me that themes are more like the root of a story, regardless of whether we do it intentionally. It would mean that every plot point, setting, character, and other aspects of a story can function as the carrier for themes.

So, themes are the root. Makes sense. This rang true for me when I was listening to *You Are A Storyteller Podcast* and one host, Brian McDonald, said that all stories spawned from the need for survival.

Archeologists studying cave paintings have suggested that these first recorded stories were ways to convey dangers and information on how to survive for future generations.

But what does this mean for us as writers in the 21st century? After all, we no longer have to constantly worry about the monsters in the long grass.

That's when it hit me: all stories spawned from the *need* for survival. The keyword isn't "survival." That was just the first topic, spawned from a *need*. "Need" is the keyword. Need is the reason stories exist.

Love, friendship, justice, war, courage. These broad thematic concepts all stem from needs we have in life. Needs we don't have, needs we have in abundance, and needs we use to attain what we otherwise couldn't have.

If themes are about conveying a need to a reader, and stories help build that need until it resonates with the reader, then we can use that to our advantage.

That's where Story Hypothesis comes in. By using Story Hypothesis as a tool, we can explore and test different ideas about our story's needs and themes.

But more on that later, let's dive deeper into the concept of needs first.

Questions:

1. Reflect on your past writing experiences. Can you identify a time when you felt the theme of your story was forced or unnatural? How did that impact your writing process and the story itself?

2. How does the idea that themes are a conversation between the reader and the author change your perspective on their purpose in a story?

3. Think about a story you've written or read where the theme resonated with you. How did that influence your connection with the story?

THE HIERARCHY IS DEAD: WHY YOUR CHARACTERS NEED BETTER

L et's face it, Maslow's hierarchy doesn't cut it. At least, not when it comes to writing a story.

A quick recap.

Maslow's hierarchy of needs is a pyramid that categorizes human needs into five levels, starting with the bottom. The idea is that we must meet the base level needs before we will desire to seek the next levels of the pyramid. From bottom to top, the needs are - physiological well-being (food, water and shelter), safety/security (protection from physical or psychological harm), love/belonging (social connection with others), esteem and self-actualization (the realization of one's potential).

A key component to character development is knowing what our character needs. Maslow has been a popular option discovering character needs because of its visual appeal, and at a first glance it makes sense - the higher on the pyramid you get, the more complex the needs become. A post-apocalyptic story might focus on things like food, shelter, and safety; while a romance novel could concentrate on those higher-level needs like belonging, love, and esteem.

However, there are some criticisms of Maslow that make it very limiting when constructing stories.

For one thing, Maslow's hierarchy assumes that once we meet a need, it all but vanishes, which is simply not true. I don't know about you, but my need to eat comes back every day, no matter if I feel like I leveled up on the Maslow's pyramid. Maslow suggests other needs are only accessible once the lower-level needs are met, but if this were true, many people would suffer emotional whiplash from swinging back and forth on this pyramid.

This ties into my next frustration with the hierarchy, it's classist. If someone cannot attain shelter, safety, or property, then Maslow would suggest that a person would not be motivated to attain self-actualization needs. This alienates so many people who live pay-check to pay-check, gatekeeping their self-actualization and creative potential. It's also wrong. Plenty of artists throughout history are lucky if they can tick off the physiological needs, and yet the works they created are still renowned today.

Furthermore, Maslow's hierarchy assumes a one-size-fits-all approach to human needs, which negates cultural context entirely. It places personal achievement and esteem above communal connections, which devalues cultures that prioritize social connections over individual achievement. Abiding by a hierarchy places the importance of one need above another, and doing this in our storytelling would diminish diversity within our tales.

Funny enough, connection is integral in nearly all these steps. Even within physiological needs. Most of us don't exist alone on a desert island, so in order to attain our physiological needs, we need some kind of mutually agreed tolerance with a community. At a bare minimum, others around you would need to tolerate your existence enough to leave you be, else your basic needs could be taken or infringed upon at any moment (making the completion of that need impossible).

And last thing I have to say on Maslow, let's talk about sex. At the bottom of the list, in the physiological needs, is sex, alongside food and breathing. Um, what? So, before having access to any other needs, like safety, emotional connections, or community, you apparently must fulfill a need for sex. This isn't an argument for a civilization's need to reproduce, this is an individual need, and it's not true. It again highlights how much this hierarchy lacks consideration of other perspectives.

Okay, so what can we use instead? Needs are important for character development. They help drive the story and allow us to know our characters better, but Maslow is not it. I could use this hierarchy while completely ignoring the concept of a hierarchy, or I can look for something else.

Well, guess what? I found something else. A framework that considers the complexity of human needs and cultural differences, at least making it easier for us writers to use.

Questions:

1. Maslow's hierarchy has been criticized as classist, and failing to consider cultural contexts. How could this potential bias influence your storytelling if you strictly adhered to it? Can you think of examples where such a bias might have limited the depth and diversity of your characters?

2. If Maslow's hierarchy devalues cultures that prioritize social connections over individual achievement, then how might you incorporate this perspective into your storytelling, especially while developing characters from varied cultural backgrounds?

SICK OF PYRAMID SCHEMES? TRY MAX-NEEF

We have yeeted Maslow out the window.

Now what?

Guess we *need* a new framework.

How about this one?

In 1986, Chilean economist Manfred Max-Neef published an article that called out his government's obsession with traditional economic models that prioritized material goods over human needs. Instead, he proposed a wild idea: what if we prioritized fundamental human needs?

Madness, but he might be onto something!

Not only was this a path for governments to care more about their citizen's wellbeing, but unlike the Maslow's pyramid scheme, which focuses on a path to higher needs, Max-Neef's model treats all needs as equal. This means we can apply it in different cultural contexts and classes without passing judgment on which needs are more important.

Not only are there nine needs, but there are also means to satisfy those needs. Instead of being an individual's sole responsibility, social groups and environments also satisfied these needs.

Well, now we're talking!

Max-Neef applies to different cultural contexts and classes of people. It not only accounts for personal growth, but how one's social network and environment satisfy or diminish needs. This means, for us writers, this framework provides a clear foundation of needs and how we can satisfy or diminish those needs personally, socially, and environmentally.

What are the nine fundamental human needs already?!

Yeah, yeah, I hear you.

They are sustenance, protection, affection, participation, understanding, idleness, identity, creation, and freedom.

We will go into more detail on each need in subsequent chapters, but here are the basics.

Sustenance is the need for physical resources such as food, water, and shelter. These are the bare necessities for the most basic form of human life.

Protection is the need for safety and security, both physical and psychological.

Affection is the need for love, care, and belonging. This need helps us develop healthy relationships and our ability to express ourselves fully.

Participation is the need for meaningful engagement with others. With this need, we connect and become involved in our communities.

Understanding is the need for knowledge and a sense of meaning. We need to have a sense of purpose and be able to make informed decisions, which is what understanding does.

Idleness is the need for rest, relaxation, and leisure activities. Probably not a need many of you think about, but no matter what, you have to recharge your batteries.

Identity is the need for affirmation and recognition. Identity fulfills our sense of self and our ability to express our uniqueness.

Creation is the need for self-expression and creativity. It is one thing to express ourselves fully. It's another to make meaningful contributions to the world and to feel a sense of fulfillment. That is what creation fulfills.

Freedom is the need for autonomy and self-determination. No matter how big or small, there comes a time where we need to make our own choices and to pursue our own paths.

Notice that Max-Neef did not include wealth, or the need to accumulate wealth, among any of these needs. However, perhaps financial security and stability fall under the Protection need.

Max-Neef's Fundamental Human Needs provides writers with the opportunity to explore a wider myriad of interactions between needs.

For example, a post apocalyptic survivor might need sustenance, but in order to do that, they have forfeit their need for protection.

Similarly, a dystopian character might have the desire for freedom, but they lack understanding. Their freedom will fail until they truly understand their circumstances.

A contemporary piece exploring a character with burnout might deprive them of the need for idleness and participation, making it difficult for them to find meaningful ways to engage in leisure activities.

Or a young adult might have the need for identity, but lacks the need for protection, which could make them vulnerable to identity-based discrimination.

Or (last example, for now. I promise) a young Tudor character may have the need for affection, but they are deprived of the need for idleness, making them feel overwhelmed by the need to be in constant contact with others.

Hopefully that gives you some ideas on how these needs interplay with each other. Before exploring more on the interactions, I want to dive into each of these needs separately, laying down the foundation and how these needs may show up on the page.

Use these next nine chapters as a reference in highlighting various human needs in different forms of media. While we go through and spotlight specific needs within various works, it's important to recognize that many narratives encompass multiple needs, especially in expansive stories. Integrating several needs not only enriches a tale but also makes it resonate more. As you read on, I encourage you to discern additional needs intertwined within the highlighted works, underscoring the complexity of storytelling.

Questions:

1. How do you think Max-Neef's framework of fundamental human needs can influence your approach to character development and storytelling?

2. Can you think of a character from your work who might have a new dimension if analyzed through the lens of Max-Neef's nine fundamental human needs?

3. How might this new framework allow for more nuanced exploration of themes and conflicts in your writing, as it allows needs to intersect and conflict in varied and complex ways?

4. In what ways do you see the concept of the environment and social network satisfying or diminishing needs adding depth to your characters and their circumstances?

SHELTER FROM THE STORM: A CLOSER LOOK AT THE SUBSISTENCE NEED

S ubsistence is all the good stuff in life: food, shelter, relationships, and all the things that sustain the physical, emotional, and intellectual self. However, it's not just about food and having a roof over our heads; it's also about discovering one's joy and purpose. Our friends and family, careers, hobbies, and other ways of finding meaning contribute to fulfilling subsistence.

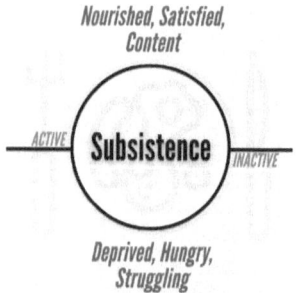

When we have enough of the basics, we experience an equilibrium in their body and mind. We're content with our current circumstances and believe we are leading a fulfilling life. This stable foundation means that some would feel empowered to take more risks to pursue greater dreams.

Without subsistence, we may feel like all hope is lost. The immediate risk of malnourishment is only one aspect of this. When we don't nourish our connections, we become distanced from our communities and purpose, which could lead to despair and depression. In a modern society, this may look like someone trapped in a cycle of poverty or desperation with no visible way out.

In stories where a character needs subsistence, such as post-apocalyptic novels, a substantial amount of effort must be devoted to finding food and other basic needs. Characters have to rely on their wits and skills to overcome obstacles and challenge themselves to find nourishment. This search has a tremendous influence on their mentality, shaping them to be more cautious and resourceful, influencing their decisions throughout the narrative.

For instance, in the post-apocalyptic novel *The Road* by Cormac McCarthy, the protagonist is desperate to find subsistence for himself and his son. This need drives the character to take risks and make tough decisions that could put his life in danger, such as entering abandoned buildings, relying on strangers, and scavenging for food. The desperate need for sustenance took a toll on the main character's mentality, making him weary and paranoid, and further intensifying his feelings of anxiety and fear.

In other genres, this might involve finding a job, connecting with others, or growing emotionally.

In J. D. Salinger's *The Catcher in the Rye*, we have a protagonist who needs subsistence. Holden Caulfield is a troubled young man who is struggling to find purpose and meaning in his life. As he traipses through New York City, Holden finds subsistence in his relationships with people, such as his sister Phoebe and Mr. Antolini. He also finds subsistence in his love and appreciation for art and literature. Through finding subsistence, Holden can come to terms with his own feelings of loneliness and despair.

In the novel *Stone Butch Blues* by Leslie Feinberg, the protagonist Jess Goldberg is genderqueer, struggling to find subsistence in multiple aspects of their life. They navigate a hostile world that rejects their gender identity, and because of that, Jess seeks subsistence through building a strong support network within the LGBTQ+ community, finding love and acceptance in relationships, and engaging in activism. The story highlights the importance of emotional and intellectual subsistence alongside physical needs, showcasing the resilience and determination of the queer community in the face of adversity.

In the film *Cast Away*, directed by Robert Zemeckis, the protagonist Chuck Noland, played by Tom Hanks, becomes stranded on an uninhabited island following a plane crash. Noland's journey illustrates the lengths one might go to secure subsistence. Using remnants of his plane and the scarce resources on the island, he constructs shelter, creates fire, and scavenges for food. His relationship with an inanimate volleyball, named Wilson, depicts the human need for emotional subsistence in the absence of real human connection. The island and his solitude act as crucibles, forging him into a man who understands the profound worth of life's basics and the human need for connection.

Alejandro González Iñárritu's *The Revenant* similarly dives deep into the theme of subsistence but is set in the freezing wilderness. Leonardo DiCaprio's character, Hugh Glass, must grapple with the harsh realities of Mother Nature as a drive for revenge keeps him alive. His subsistence is not just about survival but keeping his humanity amid the raw brutality of nature and men.

Reality television can also portray the challenges of subsistence. The show *Survivor* strips contestants of everyday comforts and pit them against nature and each other. More than the physical challenges of finding food or building a shelter, it's the emotional and social dynamics that highlight the intricacies of human subsistence. Alliances form, trust between contestants form and break, and strategies shift and change, all in the quest for the prize. What draws an audience to this show is how contestants prioritize their needs, oscillating between the immediacy of physical subsistence and the long-term play of emotional and social connections.

In the vast expanse of media, these stories of subsistence emphasize how survival isn't just a fight for the basics but often a deeper quest for emotional and psychological fulfillment. Whether travelling down a post apocalyptic road, amid a desolate island, a chilly wilderness, or even amidst deceivingly warm sandy beaches, pursuing subsistence remains a universally engaging narrative.

Ultimately, subsistence is an essential need that drives the happiness and health of a person within their community. In literature, characters finding subsistence can experience emotional growth and find fulfillment, and without it, they can feel helpless and desperate. Subsistence is essential for survival, and a fundamental part of our lives.

Questions:

1. Is this particular need a major need in your protagonist's journey and growth? How would the absence of this need affect their trajectory?

2. How does the satisfaction or deprivation of this need impact your character's actions and decisions throughout the story?

3. How does this need intersect with other needs in your character's life, and how does it contribute to the overall conflict or resolution of the story?

4. How can the struggle for subsistence provide opportunities for character growth, the development of relationships, or changes in your character's world view?

5. How might a character's societal position (like poverty, gender identity, etc.) influence their pursuit of subsistence? Can you think of ways to incorporate these influences more deeply into your characters' arcs?

You in Danger, Girl: A Deep Dive into the Protection Need

P rotection, as identified by Manfred Max-Neef, is the desire to feel safe and secure from physical, psychological, and emotional risks that lurk behind every corner. This fundamental human need plays a vital role in our well-being. Protection serves as a form of self-preservation, ensuring we can relax and scroll through social media without fear of impending doom. Unless, the act of scrolling social media causes the doom. In that case, maybe a nice bubble bath or something.

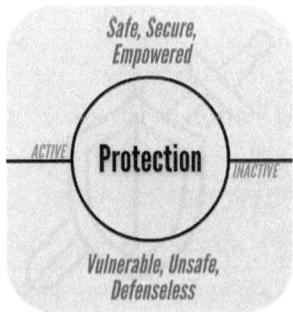

Various forms of protection exist, from the classic "lock your doors and hide your kids" to seeking therapy and working on the awareness of your mental state. Protection helps create a sense of safety, allowing individuals to feel free from worry and stress, ultimately leading to contentment and peace.

In the absence of protection, we might experience heightened anxiety, fear, and vulnerability. Actively seeking protection, whether through researching safety measures, engaging in counseling, or confiding in trusted friends or family members, no matter how daunting these tasks may be, demonstrates strength and resilience.

Protection plays a significant role in storytelling, particularly when a character requires it. Imagine a slasher thriller, where the protagonist is desperately seeking protection from a mysterious killer. This need shapes the character's decisions, leading them to avoid dark alleys (if they want to survive), stay in well-lit places, or lock the doors at night. The constant search for protection impacts the character's mentality, making them feel anxious or determined to survive.

When a character seeks protection, they may become hyper-aware of their physical and emotional state and their environment. This awareness can lead to a sense of empowerment as they take control of their safety and security.

For instance, in the dystopian novel *The Handmaid's Tale* by Margaret Atwood, the protagonist Offred constantly needs protection as she navigates a dangerous and oppressive society that makes Orwell's *1984* look like a walk in the park. Her desire for safety drives her to make calculated decisions, take calculated risks, and find allies who can provide her with some sense of protection. Offred's mentality is deeply affected by her precarious situation, causing her to be vigilant throughout the story.

In the young adult novel *Aristotle and Dante Discover the Secrets of the Universe* by Benjamin Alire Sáenz, the two main characters, Aristotle "Ari" Mendoza and Dante Quintana, are Mexican-American teenagers exploring their cultural and sexual identities. As their friendship develops into a deeper connection, both characters seek protection in different ways. Ari grapples with his family's unspoken traumas and learns to open up, finding protection in vulnerability and communication. On the other hand, Dante faces the challenges of coming out and embraces his authentic self, finding protection in the strength of his identity and the support of those who love him. The story shows how emotional and psychological protection can be essential for the growth and well-being of these characters.

In John Krasinski's cinematic venture *A Quiet Place*, they literally set the stakes in sound. The film portrays a post-apocalyptic world where alien creatures hunt humans who make even the slightest of noises. While the imminent physical threat is ever-present, the emotional core of the movie is the extent to which parents would go to protect their children. In their silent world, every whispered word, every muted step is calculated to protect, not just from the predators outside but from the constant grip of fear and paranoia. The movie showcases that true protection sometimes isn't about erecting walls but about understanding and adaptation, providing an emotional shelter for loved ones amidst external chaos.

David Fincher's *Panic Room* taps into the urban nightmares of invasion. Jodie Foster and Kristen Stewart, playing a mother-daughter duo, become accidental prisoners in their own home when burglars break in, seeking a treasure. The panic room the previous tenants had installed becomes both a physical and psychological sanctuary. Their determination to survive underscores the primal instincts of a mother's protective nature and a child's trust.

Bodyguard, featuring Richard Madden as David Budd, encapsulates protection on multiple levels. At the surface, it's about Budd's role in shielding high-profile clients from threats, but delving deeper, it's also about his personal battle with PTSD and the scars of war.

While professionally, he's the protector, internally he's in dire need of protection. Protection from his traumatic memories, his collapsing mental health, and the complicated web of politics and betrayal. This duality serves as a reminder that sometimes those who seem the strongest, those who shield others, are themselves in desperate need of sanctuary.

Protection plays a profound role in human lives, making it a crucial aspect of storytelling. It influences a character's mentality, whether they possess it or actively seek it. Protection offers a sense of safety and security, leading to feelings of peace and contentment. Meanwhile, the pursuit of protection results in a sense of empowerment, as the character takes control of their safety and security, significantly impacting their journey.

Questions:

1. Is this particular need a major need in your protagonist's journey and growth? How would the absence of this need affect their trajectory?

2. How does the satisfaction or deprivation of this need impact your character's actions and decisions throughout the story?

3. How does this need intersect with other needs in your character's life, and how does it contribute to the overall conflict or resolution of the story?

4. Can you think of instances in your stories where a lack of protection resulted in a significant shift in your character's journey?

5. Protection can be sought on many levels - physical, emotional, psychological. Which form of protection seems most relevant to your protagonist and why?

ALL YOU NEED IS LOVE: EXPLORING THE AFFECTION NEED

A ffection connects us to one another, providing comfort and security through emotional ties. This love, care, and appreciation creates that warm fuzzy feeling that gives us a sense of importance and value we all so desperately need.

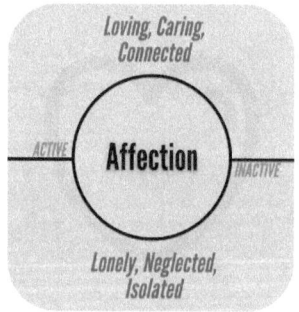

When we experience affection in our lives, we often exhibit greater happiness, optimism, and healthier relationships with others. Moreover, affection can help us cope with stress and adversity, as feeling loved and appreciated fosters hope and resilience.

Affection can present itself in different ways, from physical touch like hugging or holding hands, verbal expressions like compliments or saying "I love you," to nonverbal gestures like smiling or making eye contact. Other less obvious forms of affection may include taking care of someone's needs, doing favors, or simply spending time together. These expressions of affection may differ among individuals, but they all serve the purpose of showing others they are important, valued, and cared for.

In literature, characters often grapple with an unmet need for affection, which propels them through the plot and influences their actions. Examining how affection influences a character's mentality when present or sought after can enhance our understanding of the characters and their motivations.

On the other hand, when characters have unmet affection needs, they often encounter themes of loneliness, insecurity, or a desire for love and acceptance. This can motivate them to seek romantic relationships, new social circles, or ways to feel appreciated and valued. This need can generate tension and conflict as characters confront obstacles and hardships to get the affection they desire.

This is the drama we readers eat up!

For instance, in Shakespeare's *Romeo and Juliet*, the young lovers' need for affection leads them to defy their feuding families and pursue their love for each other. Their passion and desire for each other's affection ultimately leads to tragic consequences, showing how powerful the need for affection can be in shaping characters' fates.

In Jane Austen's *Pride and Prejudice*, protagonist Elizabeth Bennet's need for affection drives her journey towards self-awareness and love. Navigating societal expectations and her own prejudices, Elizabeth ultimately finds affection in her relationship with Mr. Darcy, resulting in emotional growth and happiness for both characters.

In the novel *Annie on My Mind* by Nancy Garden, the protagonists Liza and Annie are two young women discovering their love for each other amidst societal disapproval. As they develop their relationship and seek affection, they face the challenges of societal judgment, family expectations, and internal struggles. The affection they share becomes a source of strength, allowing them to overcome adversity and embrace their love for one another.

Affection also plays a role in the iconic TV show *Friends*. The story revolves around six individuals living in the heart of New York City, as they navigate the maze of adulthood. While there are romantic pursuits, hilarious misadventures, and personal struggles, at its core, *Friends* underscores the deep affection the group holds for one another. Their unwavering bond provides an emotional sanctuary against the challenges of city life, broken relationships, and career setbacks. The characters' dynamics, from Ross and Rachel's tumultuous relationship to Joey and Chandler's bromance, reiterate that affection isn't always romantic; it's the myriad forms of love, loyalty, and comfort we share with those closest to us.

Bridget Jones's Diary, both a novel by Helen Fielding and film adaptation directed by Sharon Maguire, gives us an intimate look into the life of Bridget Jones, a woman constantly battling societal and self-imposed standards. Amidst her humorous attempts to make sense of life, lies a deep-seated need for affection, love, and acceptance. Whether it's from her friends, her family, or romantic interests like Mark Darcy, Bridget's journey is a poignant reminder of our universal desire to be loved for who we truly are, flaws and all.

Love Actually, directed by Richard Curtis, stands as a beautiful tapestry of interwoven tales that explore the nuances of affection. From young love to mature relationships, unrequited affection to rekindled flames, the movie delves into the many shades of love. Each storyline, whether it's about a prime minister falling for his staff member or a man secretly in love with his best friend's wife, emphasizes that affection knows no boundaries, and its pursuit can lead to heartbreak or happiness, often both.

Affection profoundly affects our well-being. It helps us express our connections while making others feel important and valued. Understanding how affection interacts with a character's mentality in literature can deepen our comprehension of their motivations and actions.

Questions:

1. Is this particular need a major need in your protagonist's journey and growth? How would the absence of this need affect their trajectory?

2. How does the satisfaction or deprivation of this need impact your character's actions and decisions throughout the story?

3. How does this need intersect with other needs in your character's life, and how does it contribute to the overall conflict or resolution of the story?

4. How do your characters express affection? Do they express it through physical touch, verbal expressions, nonverbal gestures, or some other less obvious forms?

5. Can you think of a situation in your story where a character's unmet need for affection causes conflict or tension?

WE ARE THE WORLD: THE IMPORTANCE OF PARTICIPATION

D o you want to feel included? Then, participation is the need for you. When we feel connected to something larger than ourselves and driven to make contributions to our communities, that is participation. It is our engagement with others, and the world, that brings about change and revolution. Participation is the difference we make in the world.

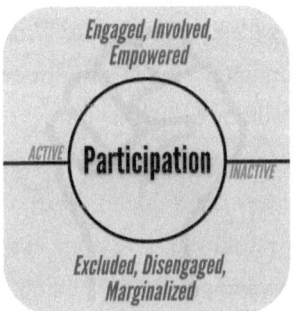

When we're practicing participation, we collaborate and engage with others. This may include anything from group projects, games, involvement with clubs or organizations, or joining social justice groups. This need drives us to engage in meaningful dialogue with others and be an active listener to each other's differences. Participation can be reflected in many forms, from sitting around a D&D table, to volunteering on a community project, or joining a political organization.

When our ability to participate is depleted or ignored, we might feel disconnected or isolated from our communities and the world. Meaningful relationships may seem fleeting, and the ability to connect with others might seem difficult. If this need is outright ignored, we might even feel like a perpetual outsider and struggle to find purpose or meaning in our life.

The need for participation in stories reflects strongly in social justice novels and dystopian tales. In dystopian stories, characters are usually pulled from their communities and environment, isolated from the rest of the world, and then disconnected from those around them. They often become an outsider in a strange world and lack meaningful relationships. However, their need for participation drives them to find purpose and belonging, which often leads them to rise against the institutions with varying results.

In George Orwell's *1984*, the protagonist Winston Smith is isolated from the world around him. He's in a later stage of dystopia, where he is an active contributor to altering history for the overreaching government. His need to participate cannot be satiated for long when a government suppresses the ability to debate and actively listen to alternative ideas. He rebels, and finds solace in a lover, Julia. Yet, his need to belong grows and grows until he finds O'Brien, who later becomes Winston's fall. This novel does not have a happy ending, but Winston's need to participate is a prevalent driving need throughout the entire narrative.

Another example is *The House on Mango Street* by Sandra Cisneros. The protagonist, Esperanza, is a young Latina girl growing up in a predominantly Hispanic neighborhood in Chicago. Throughout the novel, Esperanza sees a myriad of social injustices occurring in her neighborhood and wishes for an escape. However, she forms friendships and grapples with her cultural identity, which in part enlightens her to participate in her community. Esperanza discovers she can advocate for change in her community through her writing, enabling her to fulfill her need for participation within her community instead of alienating herself from it.

V for Vendetta, directed by James McTeigue and adapted from the original graphic novel by Alan Moore and David Lloyd, provides a powerful narrative centered on participation. Set in a dystopian England under the shadow of a tyrannical regime, the story follows V, portrayed by Hugo Weaving, a masked vigilante. V's actions aim not only at personal vengeance but to ignite a revolution. The story exemplifies the potential of collective participation, as it's the united action of England's citizens that ultimately becomes the catalyst for change.

The historical epic *Braveheart*, directed by and starring Mel Gibson as William Wallace, captures the spirit of participation against the backdrop of medieval Scotland's fight for freedom against English oppression. The film isn't just about Wallace's personal journey, but about rousing an entire nation to take control of their destiny. Wallace's rallying cry, emblematic of the power of participation, proclaims, "They may take our lives, but they'll never take our freedom!"

The television series *Mr. Robot*, created by Sam Esmail and starring Rami Malek as the lead, Elliot Alderson, dives into the intricacies of modern-day activism and cyber warfare. While on the surface it deals with hacking and the digital age's machinations, its core is a reflection on participation. Despite Elliot's personal challenges, he recognizes and embraces the need to take a stand against societal injustices. The show paints the evolution of participation in today's digital age, reminding viewers that the drive to effect change and be part of a greater cause is both timeless and universal.

Participation is a key element in how a person interacts with their community. It provides a person with self-worth and confidence, allowing them to find and explore their purpose in life. Participation gives us our voice, allowing us to grow and shape our communities into a better future.

Questions:

1. Is this particular need a major need in your protagonist's journey and growth? How would the absence of this need affect their trajectory?

2. How does this need intersect with other needs in your character's life, and how does it contribute to the overall conflict or resolution of the story?

3. Can you think of any moments in your stories where a character's inability to participate has led to feelings of disconnection or isolation? How does this influence their journey or development in the narrative?

4. How might your characters challenge or resist systems or institutions that prevent them from participating fully in their communities or society at large?

5. How can participation be used as a powerful tool for change in your narratives? Are there examples where characters have used their participation to bring about significant change or growth, either on an individual or a community level?

WALK A MILE IN MY SHOES: THE JOURNEY OF THE UNDERSTANDING NEED

The need for understanding leads us to appreciate universal truths and the perspectives of others. It gives us the ability to navigate complex personal relationships, global politics, scientific theory, and everything in between.

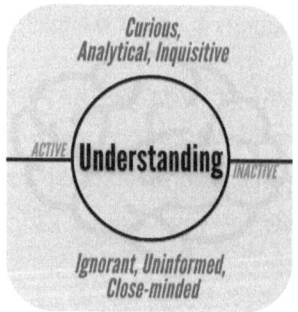

Instead of becoming a hermit and taking everything we see and hear at face value, people who actively practice understanding not only absorb information from both the past and present, but they test ideas and question the world around them. They accept some truths can change over time, and that their understanding can evolve when more information is provided. Understanding isn't a solo or siloed practice;

it requires empathizing and debating with others, building a bridge of understanding together.

When we feel fulfilled in our understanding, it's like a lightbulb goes off. We listen carefully and ask questions instead of making assumptions and refusing alternative, or even logical, solutions. If we understand, then we give the benefit of the doubt to others, instead of jumping to conclusions. To truly understand, we see the situation from the other person's perspective, not just from our own.

If we don't understand, or refuse to, then we might struggle to empathize with the other perspective. We refuse debate, and dig our heels into whatever "truth" we believe in regardless of any new information that might be better or show contradictions in our present "truth." Communication falters, misunderstandings multiply, and we find ourselves isolated or disconnected from anyone who doesn't hold the same understanding as us. Without this drive to understand beyond face value, we might become quick to judge, create assumptions without knowing, and let our emotions drive the conversation. Healthy relationships come from our differences and our willingness to appreciate those differences.

In the novel *To Kill a Mockingbird* by Harper Lee, the young protagonist, Scout Finch, embarks on a journey of understanding. She navigates the complexities of race, morality, and empathy in her small Southern town. Through her witnessing the injustice faced by Tom Robinson, a Black man falsely accused of a crime, Scout questions her own previous understanding of race and fairness. Throughout the novel, Scout's father, Atticus Finch, acts as a guiding force, teaching her the importance of putting oneself in another person's shoes to truly understand their perspective. This newfound understanding allows her to develop empathy and compassion for those who suffer injustices.

In Angie Thomas's novel *The Hate U Give*, the protagonist, Starr Carter, grapples with the need for understanding as she confronts the challenging realities of race relations and police violence in her community. Following the tragic shooting of her childhood friend, Starr is forced to reevaluate her beliefs and perceptions about the people around her. Throughout the story, Starr strives to understand the motivations and perspectives of her family, friends, and even the police, even when it is uncomfortable or painful. This journey towards understanding enables her to make informed decisions rooted in her values and beliefs, while fostering empathy and compassion for others. In the end, Starr's growing understanding of her world allows her to find her voice, inspiring her to become an advocate for change.

The film *The Matrix*, directed by Lana and Lilly Wachowski, takes us deep into the psyche of Thomas Anderson, known by his hacker alias Neo, played by Keanu Reeves. As he grapples with messages leading him down the rabbit hole to the question, "What is the Matrix?". His reality shatters, leading him into a dystopian world governed by machines, where he struggles with newfound knowledge and responsibilities as "The One." Neo's need to understand not only the world around him but also his role within it challenges him to reject the superficial and delve deeper into what reality truly means.

The intricate narrative of the series *Westworld*, created by Jonathan Nolan and Lisa Joy and based on Michael Crichton's 1973 film, delves into the blurred lines between reality and artificial creation. Characters like Dolores, portrayed by Evan Rachel Wood, an android host who gradually becomes sentient, really punctuates this story. As Dolores and other hosts recall fragments of memories and confront the reality of their existence, they grapple with the question of free will and the nature of their constructed reality. This quest for understanding underscores the broader human need to comprehend existence, memory, and the essence of consciousness.

Lost, a series created by J.J. Abrams, Damon Lindelof, and Jeffrey Lieber, delves into the mysteries of a remote island and the survivors of a plane crash stranded there. The story unfolds as the survivors, including characters like John Locke, portrayed by Terry O'Quinn, not only attempt to understand the cryptic nature of the island but also confront their own personal traumas and pasts. As each character's backstory is revealed, the overarching theme of understanding one's history and its impact on present actions becomes clear. John Locke, especially, epitomizes the journey of understanding—from his troubled relationship with his father to his faith in the island's mystic properties.

Understanding shapes a character's mentality. When a character has understanding, they approach situations with open-mindedness and empathy. They also carry with them certain truths and knowledge, allowing them to overcome obstacles and face reality. They become catalysts for change, either internally or externally, spreading their understanding and focusing on uplifting their communities.

Questions:

1. Is this particular need a major need in your protagonist's journey and growth? How would the absence of this need affect their trajectory?

2. How does the satisfaction or deprivation of this need impact your character's actions and decisions throughout the story?

3. How does this need intersect with other needs in your character's life, and how does it contribute to the overall conflict or resolution of the story?

4. How do you utilize dialogue, internal monologue, or other literary devices to convey a character's journey towards understanding?

5. How might the broader themes in your stories—such as social justice, identity, or relationships—be influenced by your characters' level of understanding? Can understanding serve as a catalyst for change within these themes?

The Sound of Silence: Finding Clarity and Perspective Through Idleness

I dleness is the state of complete physical and mental ease. It is the freedom from all tasks and temporary pause on daily life expectations. This is the need that gives space for rest and relaxation, granting us the ability to focus and appreciate the present.

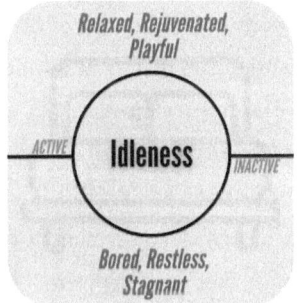

When we experience idleness, we get a strong connection with our inner selves and the surrounding world. We become content and tranquil, lost in the moment, free from distractions. Idleness brings about a clarity and perspective on life, usually establishing a bond between ourselves and nature.

Practicing idleness generally involves moments of mindfulness practices, in which we set aside time to observe our thoughts and emotions without judgment or expectation. This meditation doesn't always require sitting still, but could be a leisure walk in the woods or any means of disconnecting from the outside world and fully engaging in the present moment.

If we refuse idleness in our loves, then we might feel anxious, stressed, or overwhelmed with their day-to-day life. We might struggle to understand what we want, and might find it challenging to express our emotions. Without idleness, which grants a way to understand ourselves, we are left feeling lost and simply navigating life's expectations, subject to the expectations of others.

Idleness can be a spark for change and growth, especially in stories where a character may need more idleness in their life. Cozy novels often exemplify this, featuring characters who are stressed or burned out in their fast-paced lives. Either intentionally or inadvertently, they end up in a place where idleness is cherished, and they create a space to process their emotions and make sense of their wants in life. This pause gives them the opportunity to rethink what truly matters, and how they want to live life moving forward.

In the novel *The Unlikely Pilgrimage of Harold Fry* by Rachel Joyce, the protagonist, Harold, walks across England to visit a dying friend. As Harold gradually distances himself from the hustle and bustle of his ordinary life, he is forced to live in the moment and reflect on his own life and relationships. His physical journey mirrors his inner one, allowing him to ultimately find peace and self-acceptance. Through Idleness, Harold transforms his life and the lives of the people he meets, showcasing how mindfulness is not only important for one's personal journey but also how seeing someone self-reflect serves others.

In *Giovanni's Room* by James Baldwin, our protagonist, David, deals with the challenges of his sexuality and identity in 1950s Paris.

Idleness emerges throughout the novel as David must confront his feelings for his girlfriend, Hella, and Giovanni. Within the moments spent in Giovanni's room, David can temporarily escape societal expectations and discover his true desires. However, societal and personal pressures to conform to hetero-normative expectations continue to press down on him. This novel shows how idleness helps David see his authentic self, even in a world that may be unaccepting of that identity. *Note: here that David's moments of idleness allow space for him to discover his identity, which is another need in the Max-Neef model.*

Sofia Coppola's cinematic gem *Lost in Translation* captures the theme of idleness amid Tokyo's bustling life. The story revolves around two characters, Bob, played by Bill Murray, and Charlotte, portrayed by Scarlett Johansson. Both are escaping the monotony and dissatisfaction of their lives. Placed in a foreign land with a vast language and cultural barrier, they find solace in each other's company. Their shared moments of idleness, whether it be gazing at the neon-lit city from a hotel window or wandering the neon-lit streets, provide them a pause from their regular lives, allowing introspection and a genuine connection. Coppola elegantly depicts how sometimes, in doing nothing and just being, one can discover profound insights about life and oneself.

The Big Lebowski directed by the Coen Brothers, introduces us to Jeffrey Lebowski, better known as "The Dude", played by Jeff Bridges. The Dude's life embodies idleness. He enjoys simple pleasures, like bowling and the occasional White Russian drink. Despite getting inadvertently wrapped up in a bizarre plot involving mistaken identity, kidnapping, and ransom, The Dude's goal remains unwavering: to remain relaxed and to return to his usual state of leisure. The Dude's commitment to idleness in the face of chaos underscores the importance of maintaining one's own pace in life, regardless of external circumstances.

Parks and Recreation, a series created by Greg Daniels and Michael Schur, brings forth the character of Ron Swanson, masterfully portrayed by Nick Offerman. As the head of the Parks Department in the fictional town of Pawnee, Indiana, Ron's stoic nature is juxtaposed against his immense love for leisure. Whether it's a retreat into nature, woodworking in his workshop, or simply sitting back with a glass of whiskey, Swanson's moments of idleness are more than just comic relief. Even amidst the chaos of work and societal demands, moments of relaxation and disconnect are crucial for rejuvenation.

Idleness can have a significant influence on how we think and view life. By focusing on and grounding oneself in the present, or reflecting on one's thoughts and emotions, we can learn to appreciate the simple pleasures of life. Joy doesn't need to be forged by big events, and idleness shows a path to finding that joy in small moments, building a stronger connection with ourselves and the world.

Questions:

1. Is this particular need a major need in your protagonist's journey and growth? How would the absence of this need affect their trajectory?

2. How does the satisfaction or deprivation of this need impact your character's actions and decisions throughout the story?

3. How does this need intersect with other needs in your character's life, and how does it contribute to the overall conflict or resolution of the story?

4. How do you explore the theme of idleness in your writing? Have you created characters who have to deliberately take a pause in their fast-paced life to gain clarity?

5. In your writing, how have you conveyed the concept of idleness without it being perceived as laziness or lack of productivity? How do you highlight the benefits of idleness to your characters and readers?

6. How can you navigate the balance between plot movement and moments of idleness in your writing? What might you do to create moments of quiet reflection and introspection without slowing down the pace of the story too much?

WHEN WILL MY REFLECTION SHOW WHO I AM INSIDE: PEELING BACK THE LAYERS OF IDENTITY

When you look inward, what do you see? Identity is our core essence. It encompasses our special blend of traits, quirks, idiosyncrasies, values, beliefs, and experiences that shape who we are as individuals. Our need for identity helps us find purpose, make connections, and feel like we have our own voice in the world.

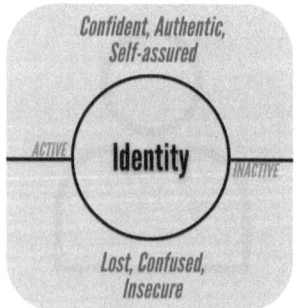

Someone with a strong sense of identity would clearly understand their core beliefs and desires at their present moment in life. They would be comfortable in their own skin, with a strong confidence in their abilities and decisions. Having a strong and defined identity allows people to find resilience against adversity, standing firm in their core tenets. Unfortunately, sometimes these strong identities can be harmful for others, especially when certain beliefs and ideals become core aspects of someone's self. Either way, identity plays a crucial role in personal development, guiding people to self-discovery and self-acceptance.

Developing a strong and healthy sense of identity often involves reflection and exploration of one's self. When we engage in activities and experiences that resonate with our core tenets, we can feel our true identities resonate. Hobbies, community involvement, connecting with like-minded individuals, or introspection are ways to help refine and define our identity. Healthy identities can evolve and grow over time, accepting that as we change and develop, time plays a role in our present identity.

When our identities are threatened or unfulfilled, we might feel confusion, insecurity, and self-doubt. How we respond to this is just as unique as our identities, spanning somewhere in the realm of hostility to seclusion, depending on the person. We might struggle to find our values and beliefs, especially if we aren't granted the time or ability to reflect and take part in resonating activities. This can lead to a sense of aimlessness or a lack of direction in life. When we lack our own identities, we struggle to relate and form deep connections with others, especially since strong relationships are built on self-awareness and mutual understanding.

Identity is a powerful driving force in most western storytelling, particularly in stories where characters embark on a journey of self-discovery and personal transformation. These protagonists struggle on the page, reshaping and defining the complexities of their identities while facing challenges and expectations placed on them by others. And there is a reason these stories resonate so well with readers, a hero struggling to live up to the standards imposed on them, and then overcoming the foe and becoming who they want to be reflects the struggles of identity that we all face as we grow and evolve.

In the novel *The Catcher in the Rye* by J.D. Salinger, the teenage protagonist, Holden Caulfield, struggles to understand his place in the world and grapples with the transition from childhood to adulthood. Holden faces a crisis of identity as he confronts the hypocrisy and superficiality of the adult world. He seeks authenticity and meaning in his own life, which ultimately leads him to accept his own limitations, embracing the complexity of his identity.

In *The Color Purple* by Alice Walker, Celie navigates the challenges of racism, sexism, and abuse in the early 20th-century American South, forcing her to embark on a journey of self-discovery and empowerment. As Celie questions societal norms and expectations, she finds strength in her identity as a Black woman, building connections with other women who support and uplift her.

In the cinematic adaptation of Chuck Palahniuk's novel *Fight Club*, directed by David Fincher, the gritty, surreal narrative delves deep into questions about identity. Edward Norton's unnamed protagonist, battling insomnia and disillusionment with his life, conjures up Tyler Durden, played by Brad Pitt, a charismatic, nihilistic alter ego. This duality represents his internal struggle to find a true sense of self amidst a materialistic society. Through underground fights and rebellious projects, the protagonist grapples with his fragmented identity, ultimately realizing the destructive potential of avoiding self-acceptance. The film underscores that the path to self-realization can sometimes be tumultuous, but necessary for reconciling our inner dichotomies.

The Danish Girl, directed by Tom Hooper, offers an intimate portrayal of a deeply personal journey to self-recognition. The film narrates the true story of Lili Elbe, a trans painter in 1920s Denmark. Eddie Redmayne's transformative performance explores the emotional and physical complexities of gender identity. Through Lili's journey, the audience witnesses the challenges, societal pressures, and internal struggles someone might endure to truly align with their inner identity. It underscores the notion that self-acceptance, especially in the face of adversity, requires immense courage and strength.

The critically acclaimed series *Orphan Black*, created by Graeme Manson and John Fawcett, thrusts identity to its forefront. Tatiana Maslany stars as Sarah Manning, a woman who discovers she is one of several clones. As the series unfolds, each clone, all uniquely portrayed by Maslany, grapples with their origins, individuality, and shared genetic blueprint. Through the clones' individual and collective journeys, the series delves deep into questions of nature versus nurture, personal autonomy, and the essence of selfhood in a world where genetic identity is shared.

Identity shapes our lives, guides our decisions, and defines our sense of self. When we engage in self-reflection and exploration, we cultivate strong and authentic identities. Identities that empower us to live our authentic lives, stand up for ourselves, and even encourage others to find their identities.

Questions:

1. Is this particular need a major need in your protagonist's journey and growth? How would the absence of this need affect their trajectory?

2. How does the satisfaction or deprivation of this need impact your character's actions and decisions throughout the story?

3. How does this need intersect with other needs in your character's life, and how does it contribute to the overall conflict or resolution of the story?

4. Have you written anything where a character's identity crisis propels the plot forward? How does this influence their actions and decisions?

5. Many writers tend to inject parts of their own identities into their characters. What are some core aspects of your own identity that you often inject into characters?

PAINT IT BLACK: THE ART OF TRANSFORMATION THROUGH CREATION

In a world without creation, nothing would exist. Creation is the drive to bring something new into this world, be it a piece of art, writing, an idea, a structure, or even life. Creation fuels innovation, societal advancement, and self-expression.

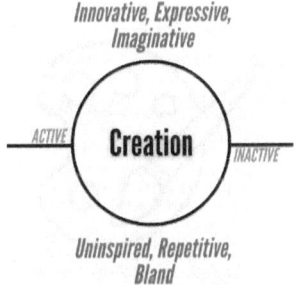

When someone embraces their creation need, they allow space for their imagination to thrive and the ability to invent surfaces. Creating brings about a sense of accomplishment and purpose, like many other needs on the Max-Neefs spectrum. Bringing something new into the world creates a source of joy and a deep sense of satisfaction as we see our ideas and visions come to life. We see our individuality reflected in the world, and we leave behind marks that we existed and we contributed in some way or another to the human experience and progress.

When we practice creation, we engage in activities that spark our imagination and encourage us to explore new ideas, techniques, or perspectives. This expands to all things tangible and not from painting, constructing, writing, to music, brainstorming businesses, or tackling a complex problem at work. Dedicating our time and brainpower to these pursuits allows our creative instincts to develop and grow, leading to more and more senses of accomplishment and satisfaction.

Stifling or hindering our creation can leave us feeling stagnated and empty. We end up disconnecting from the world around us, feeling as if we aren't reaching our full potential. Without creation, we feel stuck, living through the motions of everyday life. Without creative outlets, our mental well-being can plummet, leading to stress, anxiety, or depression.

In stories where main characters seek to bring their visions to life, creation plays a central theme. We, as readers, resonate with this need to make a mark on the world, sometimes by reading through a practical example of creation, and sometimes a more fantastical or surrealistic one.

In Mary Shelley's novel, *Frankenstein*, the need for creation drives Victor Frankenstein to unlock the secrets of life and death. Here, his pursuit of knowledge results in him creating a living being, but the consequences of his actions spiral beyond his control. What we create, and the mark we make on the world, has consequences. Some are minute, while others impact entire communities or even the world. Frankenstein serves as a cautionary tale about how our creations, especially sentient ones, cannot be controlled by their creator once they are put out into the world.

In *The Night Circus* by Erin Morgenstern, Celia and Marco are two magicians bound to a lifelong competition by their mentors. In order to compete, they must continuously improve and create various magical creations in their enchanting nocturnal circus. Their creativity and passions drive the story along, presenting various challenges and obstacles that lead to their success and personal growth. This novel showcases how creation can help shape one's identity and how it can lead to a deeper understanding of oneself and the world.

In director Peter Weir's *Dead Poets Society*, English teacher John Keating, played by Robin Williams, ignites a passion for poetry and self-expression within the hearts of his students at an all-boys preparatory school. Keating's teaching methods focuses on challenging the status quo. His lessons become catalysts for change in his students, leading them to confront their fears, societal expectations, and even familial pressures. Through the act of creation—whether writing poetry, performing plays, or simply expressing their true selves—the students embark on transformative journeys of self-discovery and growth. This film underlines how creation can profoundly impact young minds, allowing them to find their voice and place in the world.

In Brad Bird's animated film *Ratatouille*, creation finds its muse in a rat named Remy, voiced by Patton Oswalt. Despite the prejudices set against him due to him the whole being a rat and all, Remy possesses an innate culinary talent. With a desire to create delightful dishes, he creates an unlikely partnership with a human named Linguini, voiced by Lou Romano. Their journey isn't just about cooking; it's a tale of breaking barriers, defying societal expectations, and realizing one's true potential. *Ratatouille* showcases that the passion for creation knows no bounds, irrespective of the challenges one might face.

The Great British Bake Off represents the need for creation in its most delectable form. Produced by Love Productions and hosted by various beloved British personalities over its many seasons, this reality television series assembles amateur bakers from different backgrounds, unified by their shared passion for baking. Throughout many challenges, these individuals craft pastries, breads, cakes, and other mouthwatering treats. Beyond mere competition, the show lays emphasis on the joy, heart, and soul that bakers pour into their creations. Each episode, under the watchful eyes of esteemed judges, celebrates not just the skill and technique, but also the individual stories and emotions baked into every dish.

Creation has the potential to inspire, heal, and transform our lives. Nurturing our creative instincts allows us to explore new ideas, iterate on old notions, and express ourselves. That act of creation doesn't stop with us, either. Our contributions impact others and have the potential to progress humanity, pushing boundaries and forging new paths for others to embark and create.

Questions:

1. Is this particular need a major need in your protagonist's journey and growth? How would the absence of this need affect their trajectory?

2. How does the satisfaction or deprivation of this need impact your character's actions and decisions throughout the story?

3. How does this need intersect with other needs in your character's life, and how does it contribute to the overall conflict or resolution of the story?

4. As writers, we are all creators. How does your personal process of creation resonate with your characters' processes of creation? Are there any notable similarities or differences?

5. Can you think of a piece of work where stifling of creation significantly impacted a character's journey? How did you or would you handle such a situation in your writing?

UNCHAINED MELODY: THE SONG OF THE FREEDOM NEED

W e all want our own autonomy and choices. In other words, we want our freedom. This universal longing for personal liberty and equality transcends boundaries of time, culture, and geography. Freedom grants us the right to make our own decisions, to express our thoughts and desires, and is what allows us to create our own path in life.

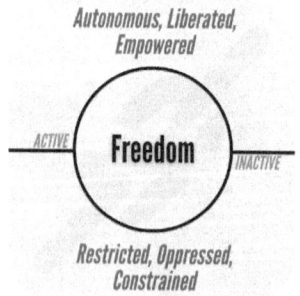

When we have freedom, we feel an empowered sense of control over our lives. We take actions, make choices and express our thoughts freely without fear of repercussion. Freedom and autonomy go hand in hand, allowing individuals to forge their future, take up space, and to make their voices heard. This need allows us to explore various facets of life, including exploring other needs without fear, and foster personal growth.

People who have freedom might express their opinions more, choose a profession they want to pursue, stand up against other injustices, or simply decide how to spend their day. Encouraging freedom in others means validating autonomy and choice, fostering a sense of self-worth and self-reliance.

On the other hand, if freedom is suppressed, it could lead to feelings of repression, frustration, and helplessness. A restricted individual might struggle against boundaries, longing for the capacity to express and act freely. Limitations on freedom can stifle creativity, hinder personal growth, and provoke a sense of despair and resentment.

Narrative centered on the pursuit of freedom reflect an innate human desire for personal liberty. Characters in these stories often battle restrictions and strive for freedom of expression, choice, and self.

Brave New World by Aldous Huxley shows a future society where people give up their freedom for stability. In this world, citizens are conditioned from birth to accept their pre-selected societal roles without question. They are chemically pacified, leading lives devoid of personal choice, deep emotions, or unique thoughts. Bernard Marx, an outlier among the conditioned Alphas, stirs up the still water by questioning this system of perfect stability. His need for freedom, in sharp contrast to the norm, drives him to question and criticize the state's oppressive control. This struggle underlines the innate human need for freedom, shedding light on the bleak emptiness of a society that trades personal liberty for comfort and stability.

One Flew Over the Cuckoo's Nest by Ken Kesey is set in a mental hospital and has a character named Randle McMurphy who fakes insanity to avoid hard labor in prison. McMurphy's struggle for personal autonomy is shown through his spirited defiance of Nurse Ratched.

McMurphy's need for freedom becomes a catalyst for change, inspiring other patients to challenge the institution's dehumanizing rules and sparking a battle of wills. His actions highlight the importance of freedom and autonomy and critique the control mechanisms that rob individuals of their fundamental rights.

Ridley Scott's *Thelma & Louise* taps into the desperation of two women seeking to break free from the chains of their mundane and oppressive lives. As they venture on an unforeseen road trip, the film unravels not just a chase from the law but also an exploration of freedom, autonomy, and the lengths to which individuals might go to reclaim their lost liberty.

Slumdog Millionaire, directed by Danny Boyle and adapted from the novel *Q & A* by Vikas Swarup, offers an exhilarating journey of Jamal Malik, played by Dev Patel, a young boy from the slums of Mumbai. Jamal's voyage from poverty to the center stage of a game show isn't just about monetary gain; it's a narrative woven with threads of love, perseverance, and, above all, the quest for freedom. Every question he answers traces back to a moment in his life, and each memory represents a step closer to breaking free from his shackled past. The movie beautifully portrays how freedom isn't just an external circumstance, but also an internal state of being.

Based on Philip K. Dick's novel, the series *The Man in the High Castle* plunges us into an alternative history where the Nazis and the Japanese Empire rule over the divided United States. Throughout its seasons, characters from different backgrounds grapple with their own interpretations of freedom in a world where it seems lost. Whether it's Juliana Crain, portrayed by Alexa Davalos, searching for truth and resistance against the oppressive regimes or Obergruppenführer John Smith, played by Rufus Sewell, navigating his own complex loyalties, the series underscores the yearning for liberty. Set against a backdrop of political intrigue, espionage, and parallel realities, the narrative sheds light on how even in the darkest of times, the flame of freedom never extinguishes.

The need for freedom is an essential component of human existence, vital to individual growth and self-expression. When given the freedom to make our own choices and express ourselves, we feel validated, empowered, and alive.

Questions:

1. Is this particular need a major need in your protagonist's journey and growth? How would the absence of this need affect their trajectory?

2. How does the satisfaction or deprivation of this need impact your character's actions and decisions throughout the story?

3. How does this need intersect with other needs in your character's life, and how does it contribute to the overall conflict or resolution of the story?

4. How have you balanced the presentation of freedom as both a liberating force and a potential source of conflict in your narrative?

5. The chapter discusses the negative impacts of suppressed freedom, such as feelings of repression, frustration, and helplessness. How have you handled these themes in your writing, and how do they serve to emphasize the necessity of freedom?

6. The chapter ends with the assertion that freedom makes us feel validated, empowered, and alive. Can you identify scenes in your own work where a character's attainment of freedom led to a sense of validation or empowerment?

THE POWER OF THREE: STORY HYPOTHESIS WITH MAX-NEEF'S NEEDS

---◄O►---

W ell, that was a lot thrown at you. However, consider those chapters as references for the future. A shorthand to human experience for crafting something that resonates.

But now we're ready to build off that and create something for our works.

Reflecting on Max-Neef's nine core needs, we should see and understand how each of them plays a crucial role in the stories we tell. These needs interplay with each other, ultimately driving a person to find a purposeful and fulfilling life. While a whole living, breathing person may encounter all nine needs in their life, I find that the stories that resonate strongest with me are stories that focus on only a few of these nine needs.

This is where Story Hypothesis comes in. Building off Max-Neef's core needs, we can create a thematic framework for character-driven narratives that explore the targeted facets of the human experience in a way that connects with our readers.

Story Hypothesis:

[Character's] need for [Initial Want] leads them to fulfill [True Need] by developing [Developing Need]

Why three needs? I have tried this with two needs before, and it also works, ([Initial Want] leads to [True Need]), but I find three create more depth for novel length work.

Let's break this down.

Often, in western storytelling, when a character thinks they need one thing, they actually need another. These could be defined as the external wants vs internal needs, where a character believes they want something like freedom, but what they really need is to participate and tear down the systems that put them in the situation in the first place so no one else has to endure what they did. However, the journey to achieve these needs can be driven by another. This need is the variable, or catalyst, that our character leans into and pushes back on, creating the peaks and valleys of a story.

> **Initial Want – External Want**
> **True Need – Internal Need**
> **Developing need – Driving Catalyst**

If we continue with freedom leading to participation, then a character might develop their protection need in order to attain this growth. In their pursuit to find personal freedom, they might struggle with what protection means to them, first protecting themself and seeing others hurt, then trying too hard to protect others at the risk of their personal freedom, before finding a balance of protecting others that fulfills their need to participate and rise up to protect everyone. Ergo, the Story Hypothesis would be:

[Character's] need for Freedom leads them to fulfill Participation by developing Protection.

Because I'm a writer, I usually pretty this up after this first step, just so I have a better emotional connection with the statement. Conveniently, *The Handmaid's Tale* would fit this Story Hypothesis well:

Offred's need for freedom leads her to fight against the dystopian society where woman's freedoms are stripped away by developing her need to protect and save others.

Especially in the TV adaptation of this novel, you can see how this statement really cuts to the core of the story, leading to moments where Offred wanted to protect her freedom more than help others, and ended up regretting that decision. Or moments when she risked her freedom too much in order to help others, and ended up in harm's way. We'll go into more of that in the next chapter.

Here are some more examples of Story Hypothesis in action:

- In *To Kill a Mockingbird* by Harper Lee, Scout Finch's need for understanding (Initial Want - Understanding) leads her to develop a sense of empathy (True Need - Affection) by using her experiences and relationships within her community

(Developing Need - Participation).

- In *The Hunger Games* by Suzanne Collins, Katniss Everdeen's need for protection (Initial Want - Protection) leads her to fight for her own survival and that of her loved ones (True Need - Subsistence) by using her skills in archery and resourcefulness (Developing Need - Creation). *Note: Throughout the trilogy we see Subsistence turn into Participation.*

- In *A Christmas Carol* by Charles Dickens, Ebenezer Scrooge's need for subsistence (Initial Want - Subsistence), which leads to his miserly lifestyle, drives him to fulfill a need for affection (True Need - Affection) by developing an understanding (Developing Need - Understanding) of the true meaning of Christmas and human connection.

- In *The Martian* by Andy Weir, Mark Watney's need for subsistence (Initial Want - Subsistence) leads him to use his scientific knowledge and problem-solving abilities (True Need - Understanding) by employing creativity and resourcefulness (Developing Need - Creation) to survive alone on Mars.

- In *Fight Club* by Chuck Palahniuk, The unnamed narrator's need for idleness (Initial Want - Idleness), as an escape from his mind-numbing corporate job, leads him to fulfill a need for identity and recognition (True Need - Identity) by developing the anarchic Fight Club (Developing Need - Participation).

Questions:

1. Looking at your current or past works, can you identify the three needs that play significant roles in your characters' journeys? How do these needs interact with each other?

2. How do these needs intertwine to create an interesting, emotionally driven narrative?

3. How do the needs develop throughout your character's journey? Are there moments when these needs come into conflict, prompting your character to make hard choices or undergo significant growth?

4. How can the needs of supporting characters interact with those of the protagonist? Are there opportunities for these characters to learn from one another or help each other fulfill their needs?

DEBATE ME: PUTTING STORY HYPOTHESIS TO THE TEST

———◆○◆———

We have a hypothesis... Now what? Well, with any hypothesis, we need to test it, argue it, and see how it stands up against all odds. As writers, we create these scenarios to support and serve as the "battlegrounds" to debate the hypothesis we created. Each scene tests the story hypothesis, with our characters either proving or disproving their own assumptions and beliefs about their needs.

If the story hypothesis functions like a debate, then your scenes serve as the counterarguments, rebuttals, and even concessions. Some scenes might support your story hypothesis, while others challenge it, leading to a deeper, richer exploration of your characters' wants, needs, and growth.

The following are the various scenes you might expect to see with most stories.

> *Warning, this may be very VERY dense, but you'll get through it and we will use practical examples in the following chapters to help break this down.*

This is also not an all-encompassing list, and some novels may not contain all these scenes. However, this should show you how the story hypothesis is used within the story.

Resistance Scene: Showing up around the 10-25% mark of the novel, the main character resists acknowledging or addressing their *initial want*. Pursuing their *initial want* would mean leaving their comfort zone, which they aren't ready for. This scene usually catalyzes change, laying the groundwork for the importance of the character's want and setting the stage for future growth and development.

Failure Scene: These scenes show up around the 20-40% and again between the 60-75% of a novel. These scenes represent moments where the character believes they have fully attained their *developing need* and pursue their *initial want*, only to fail. In the initial failures, this is usually because of the main character's presumption that they can attain their *initial want* without developing. In later chapters, these failures usually occur when the character is pushed to their limits and isn't ready. These failures are wake-up calls, forcing your character to delve deeper into their needs and growth. It's a moment that challenges the character's understanding of their needs, arguing against their current belief system, and spurring them to reevaluate their approach.

Reflection Scene: Usually between the 30-50% and again at the 70-80%, the main character takes a pause from their quest to contemplate how they have been singularly focused on their *initial want*, ignoring the crucial importance of their *true need*. These quiet moments symbolize a shift in the character's purpose, and become a subtle admission of a flawed argument and the need to recalibrate their objectives.

Misunderstanding Scene: At the 40-60% portion of the novel, the main character mistakenly assumes they attained their *true need*. The reality, however, is that they've been under self-delusion. This humbling scene amplifies their struggle, underscoring the intricate nature of their needs. It argues against a hasty resolution to the character's journey, emphasizing that the path to self-discovery still has much ground to cover.

Transformation Scene: A critical event, around 50-70% into the novel, forces the main character to work on their *developing need* to satisfy the *true need*. This is a pivotal moment in the protagonist's journey, aligned with some kind of finite end or "death" either physically, emotionally, or psychologically.

Confusion Scene: Between 60-80% of the story, the main character discovers that even though they have been working on their *developing need*, and got their *initial want*, they aren't content with the outcome. This scene leads to a reevaluation of the main character's *wants*, triggering them to prioritize their *true need*.

Revelation Scene: Around 70-90% of the story, the main character significantly shifts their understanding of their needs, realizing that satisfying their *true need* is crucial to their ultimate fulfillment. It's a moment of revelation that shakes the foundation of their earlier beliefs, offering fresh insight into their needs and reshaping their goals.

Trial Scene: This type of scene, often occurring around the 75-90% mark, tests the strength of the protagonist's *developing need*. These trials help to nudge the protagonist towards growth and self-realization. They underscore the importance of the *developing need* in the character's journey, proving it to be an indispensable factor in their self-discovery.

Confrontation Scene: Appearing around the 80-95% portion, these scenes feature the protagonist, now equipped with the full potential of their *developing need*, confronting and surmounting a significant hurdle. It's a testament to their growth and evolution, and a validation of the transformation they've undergone in their journey towards fulfilling their needs.

Resolution Scene: In the final 5-10% of the narrative, this scene depicts the main character, attaining their *true need* successfully. This scene brings the narrative to a satisfying conclusion, providing a sense of resolution and closure. It validates the character's journey, their trials and growth, demonstrating that they have led to meaningful transformation.

Each of these scenes serve as a piece of your story hypothesis puzzle. They each play a role in the ongoing debate, providing evidence, raising questions, and challenging assumptions. Sometimes when a scene feels wrong, or weak, I like to look at this list, and my story hypothesis, to see if that scene aligns. More often than not, it doesn't.

Questions:

1. Can you identify a scene in your current or past work that specifically serves as one of the scenes described in this chapter (Resistance, Failure, Reflection, Misunderstanding, Transformation, Confusion, Revelation, Trial, Confrontation, Resolution)? How does it contribute to the overall "debate" of your story hypothesis, and how consciously do you plan these specific types of scenes in your storytelling process?

2. Have you ever experienced a moment when a scene in your writing felt wrong or weak? How might analyzing it with respect to the story hypothesis and scene type lead to its improvement or better alignment with your character's needs and growth? Can you provide an example?

3. How do you balance scenes that support your story hypothesis with those that challenge it, and how do these scenes collectively enhance the exploration of your characters' wants, needs, and journey towards meaningful transformation?

4. Are there any types of scenes mentioned here that you find particularly challenging to write? How could applying the concept of the Story Hypothesis help you navigate these difficulties?

5. Can you think of a book that you've read where the author effectively used these types of scenes to test their story hypothesis? How did it contribute to the richness and depth of the story?

COZY VIBES - REVIEW OF THE HOUSE ON THE CERULEAN SEA

———◆◇◆———

R eady to put the story hypothesis to work? Let's dive into a cozy, emotional journey from the mind of T.J. Klune, and put his acclaimed novel, *The House on the Cerulean Sea*, through the ringer. Spoilers ahead, so I urge you to read this novel first before we break it down.

Set in a world both familiar and extraordinary, this tale crafts an intricate web of relationships, and questions the definition of family. Each scene of this novel creates an experiment, and with a clear theme or hypothesis, we can see how Linus's journey develops and changes. So, strap in and let's unravel this magical narrative.

Synopsis:

The House on the Cerulean Sea is about Linus Baker, a buttoned-up caseworker at the Department in Charge of Magical Youth. He leads a monotonous, lonely life, surrounded by endless bureaucracy and dictated by regulations. However, his life takes an unexpected turn when he is assigned to oversee an orphanage on an island. Linus quickly learns this is an orphanage unlike any other - it shelters some of the most dangerous magical children. It is here that Linus discovers not just a family that defies his wildest imagination but also, crucially, himself.

Story Hypothesis:

> Linus's need for Identity [Initial Want] leads him to fulfill Affection [True Need] by developing Understanding [Developing Need].

Reworking the hypothesis into something less formulaic may look like:

> By embracing our true identity, we begin to understand ourselves more, paving the way for genuine affection and love.

Now, let's delve deeper and examine the critical scenes that help debate this Story Hypothesis:

> **Resistance Scene**: Linus arrives at the Cerulean Sea and resists the idea of joining this unconventional family, maintaining his bureaucratic distance. This scene presents Linus's initial avoidance of exploring his identity, offering a logical starting point for his emotional journey.

Failure Scene: Linus's early attempts to fit in with the orphans and Arthur fail because of his lingering adherence to his old identity, which was a false identity, crafted to fit in. This scene highlights Linus's need for affection and his inability to connect with others on a deeper level.

.

Reflection Scene: Linus reflects on his life and his previously unacknowledged loneliness during quiet moments at the orphanage. This scene underscores Linus's growing awareness of his true need for affection, marking a shift in his perception of self and others.

Misunderstanding Scene: Linus misinterprets his developing affection for the children and Arthur as a professional concern. Linus is still grappling with his old identity, and this scene adds complexity to Linus's emotional journey as he starts a path to understanding himself.

Transformation Scene: The pivotal transformation scene occurs when Linus defends the children against Ms. Chapelwhite, asserting his new identity. This moment underscores Linus's growing courage and his readiness to embrace his new identity for the sake of his newfound affection.

Confusion Scene: Linus, despite recognizing his role in the family, experiences confusion when his professional success doesn't bring the happiness he expected. This scene aids the story hypothesis by revealing the conflict between Linus's old identity's wants (professional success) and his true need (affection), forcing a deeper introspection.

Revelation Scene: Linus realizes what he truly needs, which is more than accepting his identity. He needs to express his affection to others and cultivate an understanding of the strange and magical. This shift in understanding pushes the story hypothesis further, emphasizing the importance of his core needs.

Trial Scene: Linus undergoes several trials that test his understanding and determination. Three main ones are dealing with the prejudice from Ms. Chaplewhite, confronting his own fears by opening his heart, and standing up against the department to protect the children. These trials validate his developing need for understanding, reinforcing the notion that genuine change requires courage, endurance, and a willingness to challenge oneself. *Note: Trial scenes occasionally overlap with other scenes. For example, the transformation scene is a trial scene, both being an obstacle for Linus and a means to change.*

Confrontation Scene: In an emotional climax, Linus confronts the Department officials, choosing his new family over his old life. This confrontation validates Linus's transformation, reinforcing his new identity rooted in affection and understanding.

Resolution Scene: The novel concludes with Linus not just accepting his new identity as part of this family, but also embracing his role as a father figure. This resolution reinforces Linus's fulfillment of his core needs, providing a satisfying conclusion to his emotional journey and supporting the story hypothesis.

There it is, the story hypothesis in action. We explored humble beginnings, first seeds of resistance, and the emotional crescendo of confrontation leading to a satisfying resolution. Each scene mirrored the growth and transformation of Linus Baker, allowing us to appreciate how our needs for identity, affection, and understanding intertwine. Hopefully, this example demystifies how you can use Story Hypothesis in your own narratives, creating these scenes as guiding posts for your story's emotional journey.

TEACH A MAN TO FISH - REVIEW OF THE OLD MAN AND THE SEA

Let's dive into the heart of Ernest Hemingway's classic, *The Old Man and The Sea*, through the lens of Max-Neef's Needs. Again, there be spoilers ahead.

Synopsis:

The Old Man and The Sea tells a tale of an aging Cuban fisherman, Santiago, who sets out into the Gulf Stream, north of Cuba. He battles a colossal marlin, going through a grueling ordeal. This story is not only about Santiago's physical struggle but also an exploration of human nature and the essence of life itself.

Story Hypothesis:

Santiago's need for subsistence [Initial Want] leads him to fulfill his need for idleness [True Need] by developing his need for creation [Developing Need].

To phrase this hypothesis in a less formulaic way, we could say:

> Even when we fight to survive, we must take moments
> of purposeful rest, which prepares us to test our skills
> when the right time comes.

Note that creation here encompasses the development of skills, specifically testing Santiago's skills as a fisherman.

Let us now examine the pivotal scenes that debate this Story Hypothesis:

> **Resistance Scene:** Santiago, even after being unsuccessful for 84 days, refuses to give up fishing. This resistance depicts his reluctance to accept his need for idleness, or purposeful rest, setting the stage for his narrative journey.

> **Failure Scene:** Santiago hooks a giant marlin, starting a struggle that lasts for days. This scene underscores Santiago's desperate need for subsistence, and despite his initial attempts, he fails to bring the marlin on board, highlighting his predicament.

> **Reflection Scene:** During his struggle with the marlin, Santiago reflects on his past victories and failures. This quiet contemplation forces him to acknowledge his need for idleness, marking a shift in his mindset and approach.

Misunderstanding Scene: Santiago finally kills and ties the marlin to his boat, mistaking this temporary victory for his need for creation. However, this win is not yet fulfilling his core need but a step towards it.

Transformation Scene: Santiago's battle with the sharks transforms him. It is here that Santiago realizes that his act of creation is not merely catching the marlin, but his journey of perseverance against the adversities he faces. This pivotal scene stresses his developing need for creation.

Confusion Scene: Despite successfully catching the marlin, Santiago is left in a state of confusion when the sharks attack. He struggles between his accomplished want (catching the marlin) and his unexpected discontentment, causing him to reassess his true needs.

Revelation Scene: Amid the struggles, Santiago comprehends that the satisfaction of his true need lies not merely in his want (catching the marlin) but in the act of creation - a test of his endurance and the testament to his identity.

Trial Scene: Santiago's enduring battle with the sharks that relentlessly attack his marlin tests his newfound understanding. These trials underscore the importance of creation in his journey, highlighting its crucial role in his ultimate fulfillment.

Confrontation Scene: In this emotionally intense climax, Santiago, now fully realizing his need for creation, confronts the relentless sharks. Despite his apparent loss, this confrontation scene stands as a testament to his growth and his new understanding of his core needs.

Resolution Scene: Though Santiago returns with only the skeleton of the marlin, he successfully fulfills his true need. He understands that the act of creation, his enduring struggle, and perseverance have all led to a deeply satisfying resolution to his journey.

Exploring Santiago's humble beginnings, his initial resistance, and the last confrontation leading to a fulfilling resolution allows us to appreciate how intertwined our needs for subsistence, idleness, and creation are. Each scene reflects Santiago's growth and transformation, shedding light on the emotional and spiritual journey that lies at the heart of *The Old Man and The Sea*.

Dystopian Uprising - Review of The Hunger Games

N ow let's dive into something darker, Suzanne Collins's renowned novel, *The Hunger Games*. Just like before, spoilers ahead, so if you've been living under a rock, or participating in your own hunger games, consider checking out this series first.

Set in the grim, dystopian nation of Panem, this story paints a picture of survival, rebellion, and identity. And again, we see each scene serves as a puzzle piece to a larger, mesmerizing tale. With a clear story hypothesis as our guide, let's unravel the harrowing journey of Katniss Everdeen.

Synopsis:

The Hunger Games follows the story of Katniss Everdeen, a teenaged girl from the impoverished District 12. When her little sister Prim is selected for the brutal Hunger Games - a televised event where participants fight to the death, Katniss volunteers in her stead. Through strategic alliances, keen instincts, and an innate drive to protect her sister, Katniss navigates the lethal landscape of the Games.

Story Hypothesis:

Katniss's need for Protection [Initial Want] leads her to fulfill her need for Freedom [True Need] by developing her Participation [Developing Need].

In less formulaic terms:

By protecting the ones she loves, Katniss inadvertently steps onto the path of rebellion, her participation driving her closer to the freedom she seeks.

Now, let's dissect the key scenes that argue this story hypothesis:

Resistance Scene: Upon volunteering for the Hunger Games, Katniss wrestles with the reality of her situation. Despite the hardships, her life in District 12 had provided comfort. Her reluctance to abandon it reveals her deep-seated yearning for her own self-preservation, or protection.

Failure Scene: In the early parts of the narrative, Katniss strives to stand out in training to attract sponsors. Her failure is rooted in the misconception that she can simultaneously protect herself and secure freedom without fully committing to the Games. A subsequent failure occurs when she unsuccessfully attempts to ally with the Careers, underlining the limits of her participation and signaling a need for a revised strategy.

Reflection Scene: Hiding within the deadly arena, Katniss realizes her survival-focused strategy eclipses her deeper longing for freedom. As the narrative progresses, while tending to an injured Peeta, she contemplates her growing unrest against the Capitol's tyranny, strengthening her resolve for freedom.

Misunderstanding Scene: When Katniss forges an alliance with Rue, she believes she has struck a balance between participation and freedom. However, Rue's untimely death shatters this illusion, providing a harsh lesson about the true cost of freedom.

Transformation Scene: Rue's death marks a pivotal moment. Honoring Rue by covering her body with flowers, Katniss rebels openly against the Capitol for the first time, signaling the start of her transformation into a key participant in the rebellion.

Confusion Scene: Despite securing medicine for Peeta and ensuring their survival, Katniss experiences discontent. She's been participating in the Games, but it's not yielding the freedom she craves, provoking a reassessment of her strategy.

Revelation Scene: The game rules' sudden change, compelling her to potentially kill Peeta, prompts Katniss to recognize that her freedom hinges on her full participation in the rebellion, leading to a significant shift in her understanding of her needs.

Trial Scene: The confrontation with the pack of muttations tests Katniss's commitment to participation in the rebellion, emphasizing the crucial role of her active involvement in her pursuit of freedom.

Confrontation Scene: The climactic scene where Katniss and Peeta threaten to eat the poisonous berries is a direct challenge to the Capitol's tyrannical control. It showcases Katniss's evolution, her active participation now having a tangible impact on the oppressive structure she defies.

Resolution Scene: The Games conclude with Katniss and Peeta as co-victors, their threatened double suicide forcing the Capitol to give in. Having successfully participated in the rebellion, Katniss attains a form of freedom, thus validating her transformation into a beacon of hope.

From the initial resistance to the transformative moments and the emotional climax of confrontation, each scene mirrors the evolution of Katniss Everdeen. Her instinctual need for protection starts a journey that uncovers her underlying desire for freedom, which she ultimately achieves through active participation.

SILENT APOCALYPSE - REVIEW OF A QUIET PLACE

A *Quiet Place*, directed by John Krasinski, emerges as a silent scream in the realm of horror films, depicting a world where making a sound can be deadly. With creatures lurking that hunt by sound, the film unfolds a tapestry of suspense and family drama. In this chapter, we'll dissect the movie, employing our Story Hypothesis method. Before delving deeper, if you haven't watched the movie yet, be aware that spoilers lay ahead.

Synopsis:

Set in a post-apocalyptic world, the film follows the Abbott family - Evelyn, Lee, Regan, Marcus, and Beau - as they navigate a perilous existence where silence is paramount. With every footstep and whisper potentially attracting deadly creatures, the Abbotts must evolve, strategize, and above all, protect each other. At its core, the narrative doesn't merely revolve around survival but delves into deeper familial bonds, sacrifices, and understanding.

Story Hypothesis:

The Abbott family's need for Protection [Initial Want] leads them to fulfill Affection [True Need] for one another by developing their Understanding [Developing Need].

A more personal rendition of the hypothesis might be:

In times of peril, understanding our surroundings and loved ones fosters a deeper bond of affection, reinforcing our drive to protect.

Let's break down the film's pivotal scenes through the lens of our Story Hypothesis:

Resistance Scene: Early in the film, following Beau's tragic death, the family is hesitant to communicate or confront their trauma, leading to a build-up of tension. This establishes the need for protection, setting the tone for their silent struggle.

Failure Scene: Regan, blaming herself for Beau's death and believing her father doesn't love her, distances herself. Here, the lack of understanding heightens their vulnerabilities.

Reflection Scene: In the quiet moments, Lee shares with Marcus the lengths he's willing to go to for the family's safety. These reflections amplify the protection's value while subtly addressing the affection they often struggle to convey.

Misunderstanding Scene: Regan's cochlear implant emits a frequency that repels the creatures, but the family isn't initially aware of this. Their lack of understanding of the device's potential poses risks, emphasizing the journey they must undergo.

Transformation Scene: Lee's ultimate sacrifice, shouting to divert the creature's attention and save his children, marks the transformative point. His act of protection underscores his affection and the depth of understanding he's reached about their dire situation.

Confusion Scene: Marcus and Evelyn, even after discovering the cochlear implant's power, grapple with how to effectively use it against the creatures. Their attempts to derive a strategy epitomize their evolving understanding.

Revelation Scene: Regan, connecting the dots between her implant and the creature's vulnerability, realizes its potential as a weapon. This moment pushes the hypothesis, emphasizing the need for understanding in bolstering protection and affection.

Trial Scene: Evelyn, Regan, and Marcus face multiple trials – from evading creatures to ensuring the newborn's safety. These trials test their understanding of their environment and adversaries while emphasizing their innate need for protection.

Confrontation Scene: Evelyn and Regan, uniting, use the feedback from the implant to confront and kill one of the creatures. This scene manifests the climax of understanding and affection, reinforcing their protection narrative.

Resolution Scene: In the end, the family, having discovered a way to fend off the creatures, stands united. Their combined understanding and affection fortify their protection strategy, presenting hope and hinting at a resilient future.

With *A Quiet Place*, we journey through muted terrains of fear and familial bonds, observing how intertwined the needs for protection, understanding, and affection are. The Story Hypothesis shines a light on the narrative's core, revealing the emotional intricacies beneath the suspense, hopefully inspiring you to harness this method in crafting your tales.

ALL WORK, ALL PLAY - REVIEW OF THE OFFICE (US) SEASON 2

⬤

D under Mifflin's Scranton branch is a hive of quirky characters, office politics, and comedic drama. As the setting of the US version of *The Office*, its second season is rich in narrative arcs and character development, making it ripe for analysis. Let's apply the framework of the Story Hypothesis to explore the emotional journeys and core needs of the characters.

Synopsis:

Season 2 delves deeper into the dynamics of the Scranton branch of Dunder Mifflin. As relationships are explored, alliances are forged, and pranks are played, we witness how the mundanity of office life leads to unique attempts to escape it. The emerging love triangle between Jim, Pam, and Roy takes center stage, with Jim's yearnings becoming the emotional heart of the season.

Story Hypothesis:

Jim's need for Idleness [Initial Want] leads him to long for Affection [True Need] by developing Understanding [Developing Need].

Reworking the hypothesis:

In the stillness of an idle office moment, Jim seeks understanding about his feelings, paving the way for a deeper yearning for affection.

Let's break this down with key scenes from season 2:

Resistance Scene (Ep. 1 "The Dundies"): Jim resists acknowledging his feelings for Pam and maintains his composure as just a friend. This resistance to change lays the groundwork for the emotional journey to come.

Failure Scene (Ep. 3 "Office Olympics" & Ep. 14 "The Carpet"): Jim creates the Office Olympics as a fun distraction, aiming for idleness. However, he's reminded of the gap in his relationship with Pam, making the event bittersweet. In "The Carpet," Jim's attempt to enjoy an idle moment still doesn't lead to the emotional connection he seeks.

Reflection Scene (Ep. 7 "The Client"): Jim contemplates his feelings for Pam during the rooftop scene. The two share an intimate conversation and watch fireworks, making Jim realize that the affection he's been seeking has been right in front of him.

Misunderstanding Scene (Ep. 10 "Christmas Party"): Jim believes he understands his feelings for Pam and buys her a thoughtful gift (the teapot). However, he misunderstands her situation, pulling out the revealing note, thinking it's not the right time to confess his feelings.

Transformation Scene (Ep. 12 "Booze Cruise"): Jim learns from Michael that one has to seize the day. In an emotionally charged moment, he confesses his love for Pam to Michael. It's a pivotal scene where Jim acknowledges his feelings, hinting at a transformation in his understanding of what he truly wants.

Confusion Scene (Ep. 15 "Boys and Girls"): Despite understanding his feelings for Pam, Jim is confused about what to do, especially given Pam's engagement to Roy. His struggle to reconcile his idle wishes and the harsh realities deepens.

Revelation Scene (Ep. 18 "Take Your Daughter to Work Day"): Jim realizes that while he enjoys the idle moments at the office and the connection with Pam, he may need to take significant steps to change his situation.

Trial Scene (Ep. 21 "Conflict Resolution" & Ep. 22 "Casino Night"): Jim's feelings are tested when Pam's personal and professional grievances are aired out. By "Casino Night," Jim confronts his feelings head-on by confessing his love for Pam, leading to the season's most emotional moment.

Confrontation Scene (Ep. 22 "Casino Night"): The emotional climax arrives as Jim, having developed a deeper understanding of his feelings, confronts Pam about his love for her, marking a significant shift in their relationship.

Resolution Scene (Ep. 22 "Casino Night"): As season 2 concludes, the viewers understand the depth of Jim's feelings. Although it doesn't offer a satisfying closure, it sets the stage for the subsequent emotional arcs of the characters.

This deep dive into Season 2 of *The Office* underscores how even in mundane settings, our core needs (as outlined by Max-Neef) can dramatically shape narrative arcs. Jim's journey from idleness to affection through understanding offers a lens to view the complexities of everyday emotions, providing a universal touch to a seemingly ordinary office tale. Hopefully, this breakdown inspires you to use the Story Hypothesis in your analyses, allowing you to uncover layers in even the most unexpected stories.

CONCLUSION

———◆◯◆———

That's it! That's all I got for you. As you reflect on the pages of this book, I ask you to circle back on the true purpose of storytelling—reflecting human experience. This is why deriving a theme from fundamental human needs can work so well in your storytelling. Whether it's the comedic challenges of office politics in *The Office* or the profound introspections of a character like Linus in *The House on the Cerulean Sea*, stories resonate with us because they echo our desires, struggles, and hopes. They speak to the fundamental needs that Max-Neef so brilliantly articulated.

Yet, while each tale might seem unique on the surface, the undercurrents of human needs remain universal. By introducing the Story Hypothesis formula and its scene structures, we've unveiled a tool to navigate these currents, giving direction to narrative creation. Think of the Story Hypothesis as your narrative compass, pointing the way when the path isn't clear and helping ensure that your story's heart beats in rhythm with its structure.

Your Narrative, Your Needs

Now, it's your turn.

Consider your stories—those you've penned down, those in the making, and those yet to form. What are the driving needs within them? Can you identify the *Initial Want* that propels your protagonist into action? What about the deeper *True Need* that often remains concealed until the journey's climax? And then there's the *Developing Need*, the catalyst that sparks transformation and growth.

By dissecting your narratives through this lens, not only will you gain deeper insights into your characters and their arcs, but you'll also uncover the thematic heart of your story.

When in Doubt, Refer to the Compass

As a writer, it's natural to occasionally feel overwhelmed or stuck. Here is where Story Hypothesis becomes your touchstone. When trapped in the weeds, step back and revisit your Story Hypothesis. It's a reminder of where you started, where you're headed, and the milestones along the way. Or, perhaps as you've traveled deeper into your story, the Hypothesis you started with is not right, and you need to rework and revise accordingly.

Moreover, it's perfectly fine to write by the seat of your pants, letting your narrative flow without structure or outline. But then, when it comes to revise, and you see those scenes that feel weak or disconnected, Story Hypothesis is an invaluable lens.

Reimagining with Story Hypothesis

I've used the Story Hypothesis as a tool during all the stages of the writing process—whether crafting a brand new narrative, navigating a challenging scene, or revisiting a completed draft. And each time, it's provided a renewed perspective, strengthening the narrative's core.

And I've seen the transformative power of this tool in my clients' works. Whether they're seasoned authors or budding storytellers, the Story Hypothesis provides a new outlook, pushing them to reevaluate, reimagine, and refine their tales.

Embark on Your Journey

Consider this the beginning of a new chapter in your storytelling journey. Take the tools and insights offered here and apply them to your narratives. Remember, the essence of a story lies not just in its plot but in the needs, desires, and transformations of its characters.

Let the Story Hypothesis guide you through the myriad paths of storytelling. And as you venture forth, remember that at the heart of every tale lies a universal truth, a collection of human needs waiting to be explored, understood, and shared.

BEFORE YOU GO

T hank you so much for reading, and I hope this helps you with your storytelling!

Before you go, here's the deal. I'm an independent author, and reviews are the best way to help spread the word and reach new readers. If you could spare a few seconds, please consider leaving an honest review on this book's Amazon, Goodreads, Storygraph, or other pages? Your support helps so much and is greatly appreciated.

http://www.storyhypothesis.com

Sincerely,

JP Rindfleisch IX
Writer of things
Dark, Strange, Queer

ACKNOWLEDGEMENTS

Sometimes the planets align, and the right people come into your life at the right moment. I would definitely say that there was some kind of cosmic serendipity that marked the beginnings of this book and the Story Hypothesis at its heart.

Leading the charge in this journey were two extraordinary individuals, J Thorn and Zach Bohannon. Both have played the roles of mentors, friends, and champions, pushing me to question my boundaries and guiding me in the craft of writing. J and Zach, your belief in my potential and the community you've nurtured have been nothing short of life-changing.

An idea is only as good as the people who help refine it, and this book was lucky enough to have some of the best. A huge shout-out to Christine Daigle, my alpha reader, whose keen eye and insightful comments turned the raw material of this book into a polished gem. My discussions with Crys Cain about Manfred Max-Neef's needs turned into brainstorming sessions that helped mold the Story Hypothesis into what it is today. A big thanks too to Valerie Ishan and Erick Mertz for bringing me on the Writer Craft Podcast early in my discovery of Story Hypothesis. All of your continued support has been so great and I truly thank you.

Speaking of Manfred Max-Neef, his pioneering work was the lighthouse guiding the formulation of the Story Hypothesis. His wisdom resonates through the pages of this book, and I am grateful for the foundation his work provided.

Also a shout out to the *You Are A Storyteller Podcast*, hosted by Brian McDonald and Jesse Bryan, whose discussions on stories and armature (Brian's take on theme) helped create and solidify what Story Hypothesis is today.

This acknowledgment would not be complete without expressing my heartfelt gratitude to my partner. You deal with my incessant need to write early in the mornings and late into the night, and provide me with all the support and love that fuel my work.

And of course, the Author Life Community, now under the stewardship of Zach Bohannon, deserves a standing ovation. It's been a petri dish of ideas, support, and energy that has truly made this book possible.

To all who have touched this project, in big ways and small, I extend my deepest gratitude. Here's to you.

JP Rindfleisch IX

REFERENCES

Story Hypothesis owes a big thanks to the fascinating work of a Chilean economist, Manfred Max-Neef. Even though his ideas about human needs were intended as a measurement of success for a country or community, it also became a crucial part of how storytellers can craft needs and themes in their works. Below, you'll find some references that shine a spotlight on his important work and provide a path for you to dig deeper into his eye-opening ideas.

References:

Max-Neef, Manfred, Antonio Elizalde, Martin Hopenhayn, et al. 1989. "Human Scale Development: An Option for the Future." Development Dialogue, no. 1: 1.

Max-Neef, Manfred, Antonio Elizalde, Martin Hopenhayn, et al. 1986. "Desarrollo a Escala Humana: una opción para el futuro." Development Dialogue, número especial.

BOOKS, MOVIES, AND SHOWS

This book also referenced a handful of other books, movies, and shows. Here is the complete list:

Shakespeare, William. Romeo and Juliet. Various Publishers, Various Years.

Lee, Harper. To Kill a Mockingbird. J. B. Lippincott & Co., 1960.

Tolkien, J.R.R. The Lord of the Rings. Allen & Unwin, 1954-1955.

Orwell, George. 1984. Secker & Warburg, 1949.

Green, John. The Fault in Our Stars. Dutton Books, 2012.

Salinger, J.D. The Catcher in the Rye. Little, Brown and Company, 1951.

Feinberg, Leslie. Stone Butch Blues. Firebrand Books, 1993.

Zemeckis, Robert, dir. Cast Away. 20th Century Fox, 2000. Film.

Iñárritu, Alejandro G., dir. *The Revenant.* 20th Century Fox, 2015. Film.

Burnett, Mark, prod. *Survivor.* CBS, 2000-present. Television.

Atwood, Margaret. *The Handmaid's Tale.* McClelland and Stewart, 1985.

Sáenz, Benjamin Alire. *Aristotle and Dante Discover the Secrets of the Universe.* Simon & Schuster Books for Young Readers, 2012.

Krasinski, John, dir. *A Quiet Place.* Paramount Pictures, 2018. Film.

Fincher, David, dir. *Panic Room.* Columbia Pictures, 2002. Film.

Mercurio, Jed, creator. *Bodyguard.* BBC, 2018. Television.

Austen, Jane. *Pride and Prejudice.* T. Egerton, 1813.

Garden, Nancy. *Annie on My Mind.* Farrar, Straus and Giroux, 1982.

Crane, David, and Marta Kauffman, creators. *Friends.* NBC, 1994-2004. Television.

Maguire, Sharon, dir. *Bridget Jones's Diary.* Universal Pictures, 2001. Film.

Fielding, Helen. *Bridget Jones's Diary.* Penguin Books, 1996.

Curtis, Richard, dir. Love Actually. Universal Pictures, 2003. Film.

Cisneros, Sandra. The House on Mango Street. Arte Público Press, 1984.

McTeigue, James, dir. V for Vendetta. Warner Bros. Pictures, 2006. Film.

Moore, Alan. V for Vendetta. Vertigo, 1988.

Gibson, Mel, dir. Braveheart. Paramount Pictures, 1995. Film.

Esmail, Sam, creator. Mr. Robot. USA Network, 2015-2019. Television.

Thomas, Angie. The Hate U Give. Balzer + Bray, 2017.

Wachowski, Lana, and Lilly Wachowski, dirs. The Matrix. Warner Bros., 1999. Film.

Nolan, Jonathan, and Lisa Joy, creators. Westworld. HBO, 2016-present. Television.

Abrams, J.J., Damon Lindelof, and Jeffrey Lieber, creators. Lost. ABC, 2004-2010. Television.

Joyce, Rachel. The Unlikely Pilgrimage of Harold Fry. Doubleday, 2012.

Baldwin, James. Giovanni's Room. Dial Press, 1956.

Coppola, Sofia, dir. Lost in Translation. Focus Features, 2003. Film.

Coen, Joel and Ethan Coen, dirs. The Big Lebowski. Gramercy Pictures, 1998. Film.

Daniels, Greg, and Michael Schur, creators. Parks and Recreation. NBC, 2009-2015. Television.

Walker, Alice. The Color Purple. Harcourt, 1982.

Fincher, David, dir. Fight Club. 20th Century Fox, 1999. Film.

Palahniuk, Chuck. Fight Club. W.W. Norton & Company, 1996.

Hooper, Tom, dir. The Danish Girl. Focus Features, 2015. Film.

Manson, Graeme, and John Fawcett, creators. Orphan Black. BBC America, 2013-2017. Television.

Shelley, Mary. Frankenstein. Lackington, Hughes, Harding, Mavor, & Jones, 1818.

Morgenstern, Erin. The Night Circus. Doubleday, 2011.

Weir, Peter, dir. Dead Poets Society. Touchstone Pictures, 1989. Film.

Bird, Brad, dir. Ratatouille. Pixar, 2007. Film.

Perkins, Sue, and Mel Giedroyc, hosts. The Great British Bake Off. BBC, 2010-present. Television.

Huxley, Aldous. Brave New World. Chatto & Windus, 1932.

Kesey, Ken. One Flew Over the Cuckoo's Nest. Viking Press, 1962.

Scott, Ridley, dir. Thelma & Louise. Metro-Goldwyn-Mayer, 1991. Film.

Boyle, Danny, dir. Slumdog Millionaire. Warner Bros. Pictures, 2008. Film.

Swarup, Vikas. Q & A. Doubleday, 2005.

Spotnitz, Frank, creator. The Man in the High Castle. Amazon Prime, 2015-2019. Television.

Dick, Philip K. The Man in the High Castle. Putnam, 1962.

Collins, Suzanne. The Hunger Games. Scholastic, 2008.

Dickens, Charles. A Christmas Carol. Chapman & Hall, 1843.

Weir, Andy. The Martian. Crown Publishing Group, 2014.

Palahniuk, Chuck. Fight Club. W. W. Norton, 1996.

Klune, TJ. The House on the Cerulean Sea. Tor Books, 2020.

Hemingway, Ernest. The Old Man and the Sea. Charles Scribner's Sons, 1952.

Daniels, Greg. The Office (Season 2). NBC, 2005-2006.

ABOUT THE AUTHOR

JP Rindfleisch is the curator of things dark, strange, and queer. Back in the mid 2010s, amid aspirations of climbing the corporate ladder, a simple course exercise forced them to confront personal priorities. When instructed to write the things they *didn't have time* for, others in the class listed mundane household tasks, but JP wrote writing and art. The epiphany that they were suppressing their creative spirit came when they were forced to say, out loud, that they *didn't want to* write or do art.

Certified as a Three Story Method editor under the guidance of J Thorn and a Dialogue Doctor Editor within Jeff Elkins' community, JP's commitment to the craft is unwavering. Their works include *Mandrake Manor*, an LGBT Cozy Suburban Fantasy, *NRDS:*

National Recently Deceased Services, a Paranormal Comedy co-authored with Jeff Elkins, and the *Leah Ackerman Series*, a Paranormal Academy Urban Fantasy co-authored with A.B. Cohen. Alongside these, their ongoing serial *Mosswood Apothecary* offers readers a dose of LGBT Cozy Fantasy.

JP has a firm belief that writing isn't a solitary venture. It's in communities, such as the one they spearhead with the Rockford Area Writers group, that JP believes writers truly flourish.

Inspired by a desire to see authentic representation, JP focuses primarily on crafting queer fiction—the stories a younger JP longed to read growing up.

To follow JP's journey and explore their varied works, visit www. jprindfleischix.com.